Spot the Differences

Turtle or Tortoise?

by Jamie Rice

Bullfrog Books

Ideas for Parents and Teachers

Bullfrog Books let children practice reading informational text at the earliest reading levels. Repetition, familiar words, and photo labels support early readers.

Before Reading

- Discuss the cover photo. What does it tell them?

- Look at the picture glossary together. Read and discuss the words.

Read the Book

- "Walk" through the book and look at the photos. Let the child ask questions. Point out the photo labels.

- Read the book to the child, or have him or her read independently.

After Reading

- Prompt the child to think more. Ask: What did you know about turtles and tortoises before reading this book? What more would you like to learn?

Bullfrog Books are published by Jump!
5357 Penn Avenue South
Minneapolis, MN 55419
www.jumplibrary.com

Library of Congress Cataloging-in-Publication Data

Names: Rice, Jamie, author.
Title: Turtle or tortoise? / by Jamie Rice.
Description: Bullfrog books.
Minneapolis, MN: Jump!, Inc., [2022]
Series: Spot the differences
Includes index. | Audience: Ages 5–8
Identifiers: LCCN 2021028544 (print)
LCCN 2021028545 (ebook)
ISBN 9781636903521 (hardcover)
ISBN 9781636903538 (paperback)
ISBN 9781636903545 (ebook)
Subjects: LCSH: Turtle—Juvenile literature.
Testudinidae—Juvenile literature.
Classification: LCC QL666.C5 R525 2022 (print)
LCC QL666.C5 (ebook)
DDC 597.92—dc23
LC record available at https://lccn.loc.gov/2021028544
LC ebook record available at https://lccn.loc.gov/2021028545

Editor: Jenna Gleisner
Designer: Michelle Sonnek

Photo Credits: Mr. SUTTIPON YAKHAM/Shutterstock, cover (left), 21; Olga Popova/Shutterstock, cover (right), 1 (right); Studio Empreinte/Shutterstock, 1 (left); seasoning_17/Shutterstock, 3, 8–9, 23bl; a_v_d/Shutterstock, 4; Cici D/Shutterstock, 5; Murilo Mazzo/Shutterstock, 6–7 (top); Gary Stone/Shutterstock, 6–7 (bottom), 23tr; Sabine Thallinger/Shutterstock, 10–11; damann/Shutterstock, 12–13, 23tl, 23br; Alberto Loyo/Shutterstock, 14–15; David A. Northcott/Getty, 16–17; imagebroker/Alamy, 18–19; photomaster/Shutterstock, 20; mirceax/iStock, 22 (left); EcoPrint/Shutterstock, 22 (right); Mariyana M/Shutterstock, 24 (front); think4photop/Shutterstock, 24 (back).

Printed in the United States of America at Corporate Graphics in North Mankato, Minnesota.

Table of Contents

How to Use This Book

In this book, you will see pictures of both turtles and tortoises. Can you tell which one is in each picture?

Hint: You can find the answers if you flip the book upside down!

This is a turtle.

This is a tortoise.

Both are reptiles.

They look alike.

But they are
not the same.

Can you spot
the differences?

shell

Both have shells.

Turtle shells
are flat.

Tortoise shells
are round.

Which is this?

Turtles go in water.

They swim.

Tortoises stay on land.

Which is this?

claw

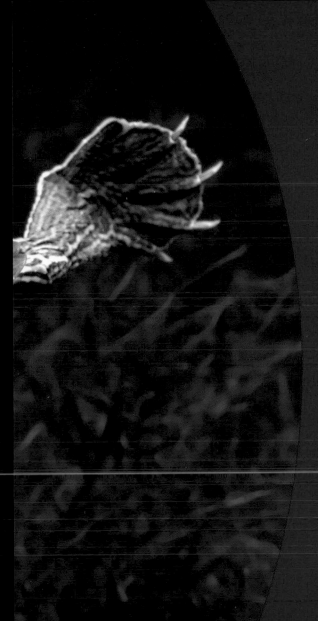

Both have claws.
Turtles have webbed feet.

Tortoises do not.

Which is this?

A turtle's legs are like paddles.

A tortoise's legs are heavy. They help it walk.

Which is this?

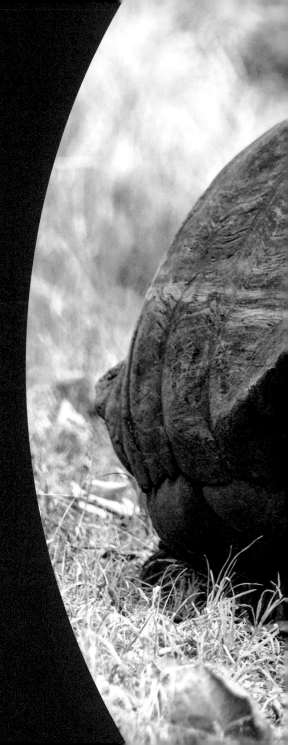

Answer: tortoise

Both eat plants.

Turtles also eat meat.

Which is this?

Answer: turtle

worm

baby

Both lay eggs.

Tortoise moms stay with their babies.

Turtle moms do not.

Which is this?

Answer: tortoise

See and Compare

flat shell

paddle-like legs

webbed feet

claws

round shell

round, thick legs

flat feet

claws

Quick Facts

Turtles and tortoises are both reptiles. They both have shells and move slowly. They are similar, but they have differences. Take a look!

Turtles

- live in water and on land
- most eat plants and meat
- mothers lay eggs and leave babies on their own

Tortoises

- live only on land
- most eat only plants
- mothers lay eggs and care for babies

Picture Glossary

claws
Hard, sharp nails on the feet of some animals.

reptiles
Cold-blooded animals that crawl or creep across the ground on short legs.

shells
Hard outer coverings.

webbed
Connected by a web or fold of skin.

Index

To Learn More

Finding more information is as easy as 1, 2, 3.

❶ Go to www.factsurfer.com

❷ Enter "turtleortortoise?" into the search box.

❸ Choose your book to see a list of websites.